African ANIMALS

DOT-TO-DOT

Evan & Lael Kimble
Illustrated by Nancy Harrison

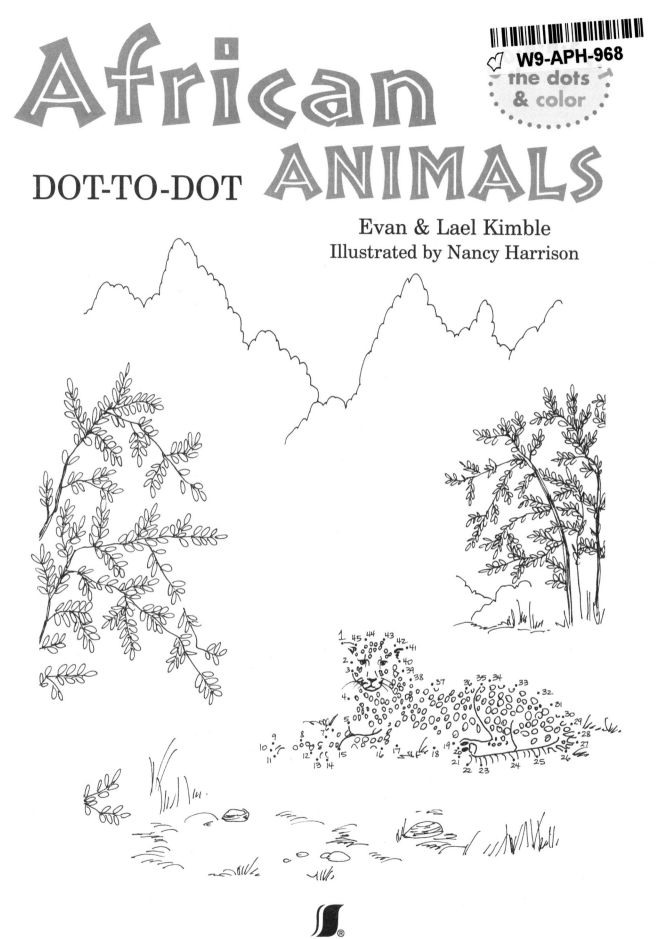

Sterling Publishing Co., Inc.
New York

2 4 6 8 10 9 7 5 3

Published by Sterling Publishing Co., Inc.
387 Park Avenue South, New York, NY 10016
© 2005 by Evan & Lael Kimble
Distributed in Canada by Sterling Publishing
c/o Canadian Manda Group, 165 Dufferin Street
Toronto, Ontario, Canada M6K 3H6
Distributed in Great Britain and Europe by Chris Lloyd at Orca Book
Services, Stanley House, Fleets Lane, Poole BH15 3AJ, England
Distributed in Australia by Capricorn Link (Australia) Pty. Ltd.
P.O. Box 704, Windsor, NSW 2756, Australia

Sterling ISBN 1-4027-2343-1

For information about custom editions, special sales, premium and
corporate purchases, please contact Sterling Special Sales
Department at 800-805-5489 or specialsales@sterlingpub.com.

CONTENTS

Aardvark

Type of animal:	Mammal
Swahili name:	*Muhunga*
Scientific name:	*Orycteropus afer*
Size:	The aardvark is 60 to 72 inches (152–183 cm) long, including a 24-inch (61 cm) tail; it weighs up to 140 pounds (63 kg)
Where it lives:	African savannas, open grasslands, woodlands, and scrub

The aardvark is a hairy, shy, nocturnal animal. (*Nocturnal* means it's active at night and sleeps during the day.) The word *aardvark* means "earth pig" in Afrikaans, a language of South Africa. These mammals eat insects, mostly ants and termites. They have good senses of smell and hearing, and they can live for up to 23 years in captivity.

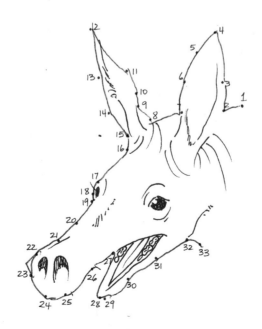

AFRICAN WILD DOG

TYPE OF ANIMAL:	Mammal
SWAHILI NAME:	*Mbwa mwitu*
SCIENTIFIC NAME:	*Lycaon pictus* (meaning "painted wolf")
SIZE:	The wild dog stands 30 inches (76 cm) tall at the shoulder; it weighs 55 to 70 pounds (25–32 kg)
WHERE IT LIVES:	Dense forests to open plains

Also called hunting dogs, African wild dogs live in packs of 6 to 20 individuals and hunt together. They usually move over a range that might cover up to 900 square miles (2,331 sq km). Their preferred foods include gazelles and other antelopes, along with warthogs, wildebeest calves, rats, and birds. These mammals can live for 10 to 12 years.

BABOON

TYPE OF ANIMAL:	Primate
SWAHILI NAME:	*Nyani*
SCIENTIFIC NAMES:	*Papiocynocephalus anubis* (olive baboon); *P. cynocephalus* (yellow baboon)
SIZE:	The baboon measures 14 to 30 inches (36–76 cm) at the shoulder; it weighs 50 to 100 pounds (23–45 kg).
WHERE IT LIVES:	Savannas and woodlands

Of all the primates in East Africa, the baboon interacts the most with people. It lives 20 to 30 years. Grass makes up a large part of its diet, along with other plant materials. Baboons also eat insects and small quantities of meat.

Baboons communicate with each other using more than 30 vocalizations that range from grunts to barks to screams. They also use gestures—yawning, smacking their lips, and shrugging their shoulders.

BAT

TYPE OF ANIMAL: Mammal

SWAHILI NAME: *Popo*

SCIENTIFIC NAME: *Eidolon helvum* (straw-colored fruit bat)

SIZE: This bat measures 60 to 72 inches (152–183 cm) from wing tip to wing tip; it weighs 9 to 11 ounces (255–312 g).

WHERE IT LIVES: Forests and savannas. Bats inhabit almost every part of the world except deserts and extreme polar regions.

After rodents, bats are the most numerous mammals on earth. They're also the only mammals that have wings and can really fly. Bats are nocturnal, eating insects, fruit, pollen, and nectar at night then hanging upside down in the branches of trees during the day. They have a great sense of smell and large eyes that give them good night vision. The fruit bat lives for 20 to 30 years.

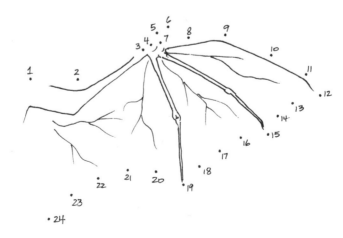

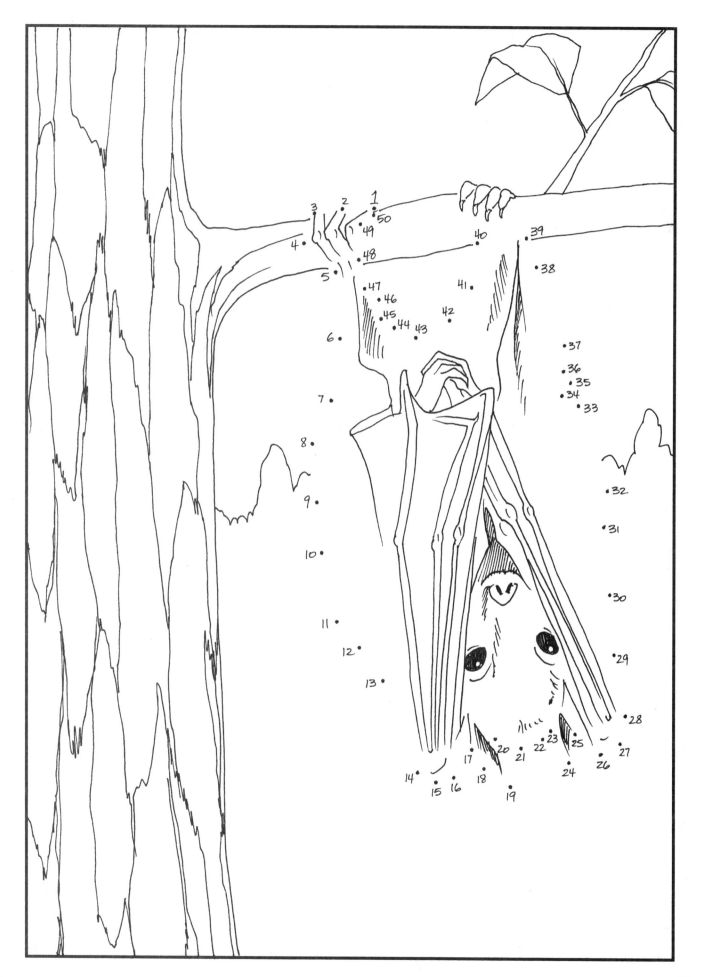

BONGO

TYPE OF ANIMAL:	Mammal
SWAHILI NAME:	*Bongo*
SCIENTIFIC NAME:	*Boocerus euryceros*
SIZE:	The bongo stands 50 inches (127 cm) at the shoulder; it weighs 500 to 900 pounds (227–409 kg).
WHERE IT LIVES:	Dense forest

A type of antelope, the bongo has lived up to 19.5 years in captivity. It eats a variety of plants; bamboo is a favorite at the right times of year. Both males and females have horns. Because they don't give off any odors, they rely heavily on their other senses—especially their sense of hearing.

BONOBO

TYPE OF ANIMAL:	Primate
SWAHILI NAME:	*Sokwe*
SCIENTIFIC NAME:	*Pan paniscus*
SIZE:	The bonobo grows up to 48 inches (122 cm) tall and weighs 65 to 85 pounds (30–39 kg).
WHERE IT LIVES:	Lowland rain forests

Like chimpanzees, the fruit-eating bonobos are closely related to humans; 98.4 percent of our genes match. This similarity has long been acknowledged by indigenous peoples of the area, who have shared their homeland with these large primates for thousands of years. Tribal legends tell of a bonobo saving a man's life, of how the bonobos showed humans which forest fruits were good to eat, and of how bonobos have tried to become human.

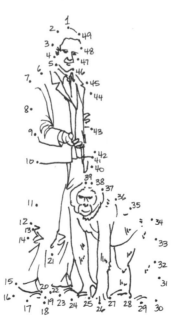

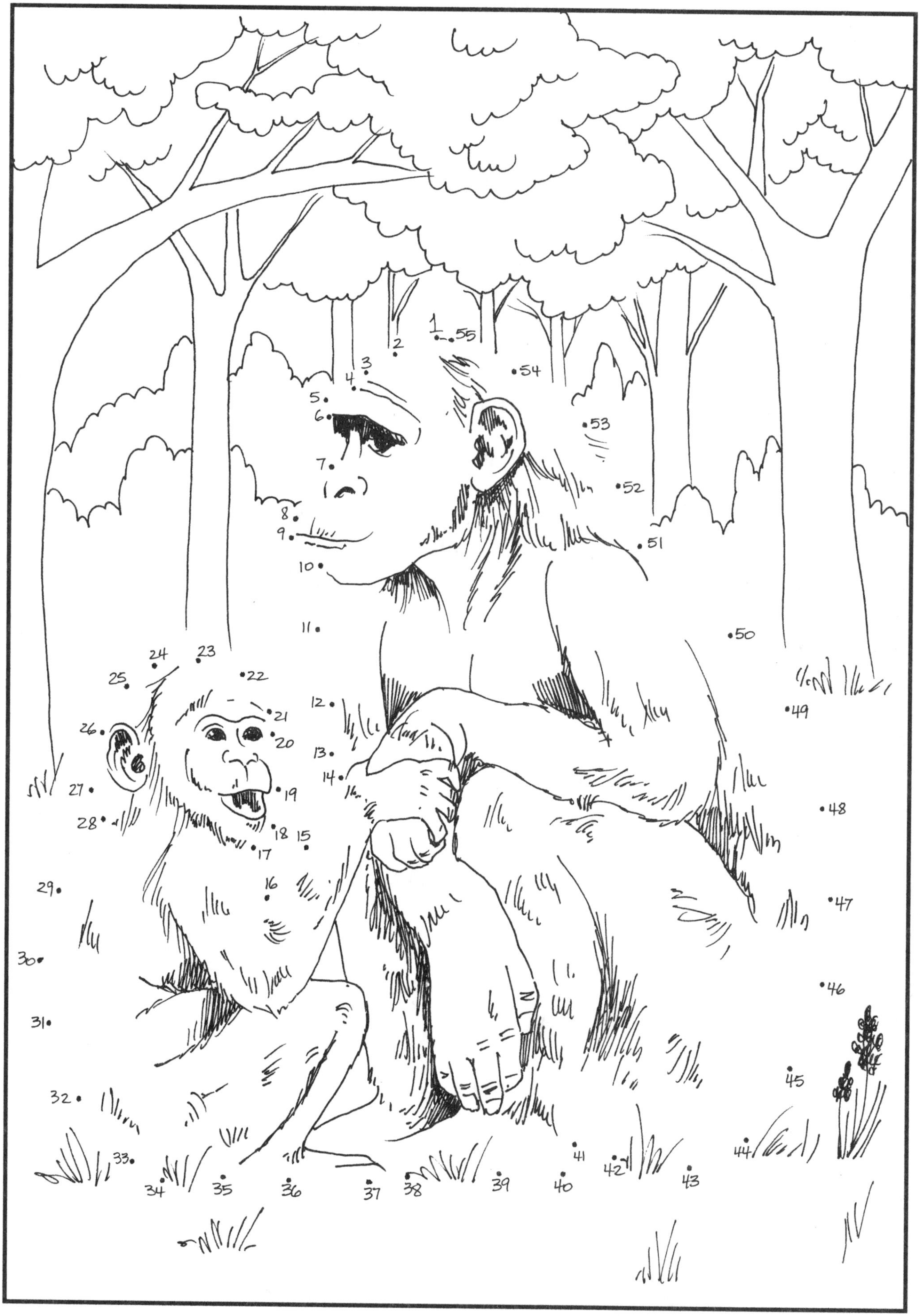

BUFFALO

TYPE OF ANIMAL: Mammal

SWAHILI NAME: *Nyati*

SCIENTIFIC NAME: *Syncerus caffer*

SIZE: The buffalo reaches about 65 inches (165 cm) at the shoulder; it weighs 1,500 pounds (681 kg).

WHERE IT LIVES: Dense forest to open plains

Also called African buffalo and Cape buffalo, these mammals live for up to 20 years. They eat grass, feeding mostly at night; in the heat of the day, you're most likely to find them staying cool by wallowing in the mud. These are among the most dangerous animals in the world, and sometimes attack without provocation.

BUSH BABY

TYPE OF ANIMAL: Mammal

SWAHILI NAME: *Komba*

SCIENTIFIC NAME: *Galago senegalensis*

SIZE: A bush baby's head and body are 5 inches (13 cm) long, and its tail measures 6 to 16 inches (15–41 cm); it weighs 5 to 10 ounces (150–300 g).

WHERE IT LIVES: Savanna and woodland habitats

This nocturnal mammal lives up to 16 years and feeds on insects, flowers, pollen, honey, seeds, fruit, lizards, mice, and nestlings. The bush baby can jump great distances—more than 20 feet (6 m)—seeming to fly from tree to tree.

CHEETAH

TYPE OF ANIMAL:	Mammal
SWAHILI NAME:	*Duma*
SCIENTIFIC NAME:	*Acinonyx jubatus*
SIZE:	The cheetah stands 30 inches (76 cm) tall at the shoulder; it weighs 110 to 140 pounds (50–64 kg).
WHERE IT LIVES:	Open savanna

A type of cat, the cheetah lives for 10 to 20 years and feeds on smaller antelopes. Cheetah mothers spend a long time teaching their young how to hunt. Small live antelopes are brought back to the cubs and released so they can chase and catch them.

The cheetah can reach speeds of up to 70 miles (113 km) per hour for short periods of time. That's faster than your car goes on the highway!

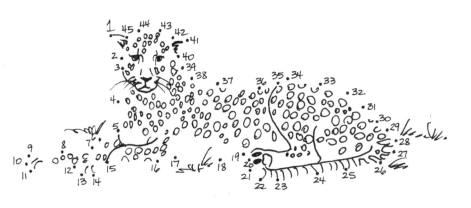

21

DIK-DIK

TYPE OF ANIMAL: Mammal

SWAHILI NAME: *Digidigi*

SCIENTIFIC NAME: *Madoqua kirkii*

SIZE: The dik-dik stands 14 to 16 inches (36–41 cm) tall at the shoulder; it weighs 10 to 12 pounds (4.5–5.5 kg).

WHERE IT LIVES: Dense forests to open plains

This tiny antelope—it's about the size of a hare—lives 3 to 4 years in the wild, and up to 10 years in captivity. It eats foliage, shoots, fruit, and berries. When a dik-dik is frightened, it makes a whistling noise through its nose that sounds like *zik-zik*—that's how it got its name!

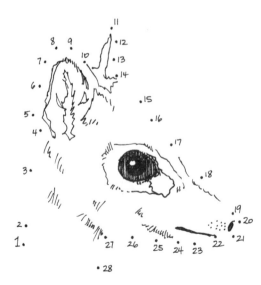

DWARF MONGOOSE

TYPE OF ANIMAL: Mammal

SWAHILI NAME: *Nguchiro*

SCIENTIFIC NAME: *Helogale parvula*

SIZE: About 8 to 12 inches (20–30 cm) long, the dwarf mongoose weighs 1 pound (0.5 kg).

WHERE IT LIVES: Forest and semi-arid areas throughout most of Africa

While they feed mainly on insects such as termites, locusts, beetles, grubs, and spiders, dwarf mongooses also eat small rodents, reptiles, young birds, and even some fruits. With a life span of about 8 years, they live in packs of 12 to 15 individuals. Each pack ranges over an area of about 75 acres (30 hectares) that usually contains 20 or more termite mounds. In addition to serving as mongoose "snack bars," these mounds are used as den sites and lookout posts.

ELAND

TYPE OF ANIMAL: Mammal

SWAHILI NAME: *Pofu*

SCIENTIFIC NAME: *Taurotragus oryx*
(Cape eland)

SIZE: The eland stands about 70 inches (178 cm) tall; it weighs 1,300 to 1,500 pounds (590–681 kg).

WHERE IT LIVES: Grassland, mountain, subdesert, savanna, and woodland areas

These cowlike mammals—the largest of the antelopes— eat plant material ranging from grass to leaves, fruits, bulbs, and roots. They live 15 to 20 years. Female elands like to keep moving, especially in the dry season, when they might travel over a 500-square-mile (1,295 sq km) area. The more sedentary males usually stay year-round in a small home range that has food and water available. They do not establish territories.

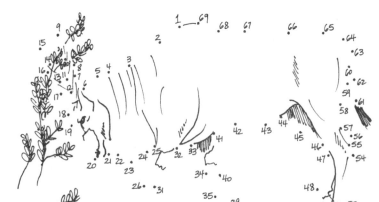

ELEPHANT

TYPE OF ANIMAL:	Mammal
SWAHILI NAMES:	*Tembo, ndovo*
SCIENTIFIC NAME:	*Loxodonta africana*
SIZE:	Up to 11 feet (3.4 m) tall, the elephant weighs 7,000 to 13,200 pounds (3,178–5,993 kg).
WHERE IT LIVES:	Rain forests, mountain forests, forested savanna, and subdesert areas

The largest living land mammals, elephants live 60 to 70 years and feed on grass, leaves, twigs, bark, fruit, and seedpods. They communicate with one another in a variety of ways. When a group of elephants is alarmed, they make earsplitting blasts and form a protective circle around the younger members. They also make low-frequency calls—so low that humans can't hear them, although they're very loud. These sounds allow elephants to "talk" at distances of 5 or 6 miles (8–10 km).

ELEPHANT SHREW

TYPE OF ANIMAL:	Mammal
SWAHILI NAME:	*Njule*
SCIENTIFIC NAME:	*Rhynchocyon cirnei* (checkered elephant shrew)
SIZE:	The elephant shrew is 9 to 12 inches (23–30 cm) long, not including the tail; it weighs 1.0 to 1.5 pounds (0.5–0.7 kg).
WHERE IT LIVES:	Dense forest to open plains

A type of rodent, this insect eater lives for 3 or 4 years. Both male and female shrews live up to their reputation for "shrewishness." They are feisty animals that will scream, spar, snap, and kick in a tumbling blur of motion. Some of their bursts of activity take place for no apparent reason—or at least for reasons known only to elephant shrews.

31

GENET

TYPE OF ANIMAL:	Mammal
SWAHILI NAME:	*Kanu*
SCIENTIFIC NAME:	*Genetta tigrina* (large spotted genet)
SIZE:	The genet stands 20 inches (51 cm) tall and weighs 4.5 pounds (2 kg).
WHERE IT LIVES:	Various habitats all over Africa

Although it is catlike in appearance and habits, the genet is actually a member of the same family as civets and mongooses. While the civet and mongoose species live mainly on the ground, however, the genet lives up in the trees. It feeds on small mammals (especially rodents, shrews, and bats); birds and their eggs; insects (frogs, millipedes, and centipedes); scorpions; and various fruits. Its life span is about 8 years.

The ancient Egyptians kept genets as rat-catching pets, and modern North Africans still do.

33

GIRAFFE

TYPE OF ANIMAL: Mammal

SWAHILI NAME: *Twiga*

SCIENTIFIC NAME: *Giraffa camelopardalis*

SIZE: The giraffe stands 18 feet (5.5 m) tall; it weighs up to 3,000 pounds (1,362 kg).

WHERE IT LIVES: In the dry savanna wherever there are trees

The giraffe's scientific name translates as "camel leopard," and this plant eater was once believed to be a cross between a camel and a leopard (it isn't!). The giraffe's neck is so long that the animal must spread its legs apart to get its head down to drink. It lives for up to 25 years.

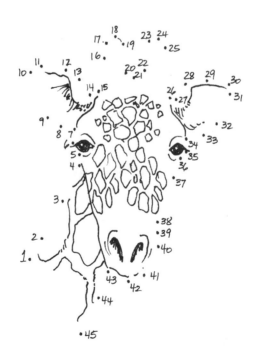

HEDGEHOG

TYPE OF ANIMAL: Mammal

SWAHILI NAME: *Kalunguyeye*

SCIENTIFIC NAME: *Atelerix albiventris*

SIZE: The hedgehog is 7 to 9 inches (18–23 cm) tall; it weighs 1 to 2 pounds (0.5–1.0 kg).

WHERE IT LIVES: In many different climates in East Africa, and over much of the world, but not in the Americas

Hedgehogs are nocturnal mammals that sleep most of the day, then spend their nights feeding on insects, snails and slugs, eggs, small mammals, ground-nesting birds, frogs, reptiles, fruit, fungi, and roots. Some species hibernate in winter; others spend the hot, dry African summer sleeping or at least remaining inactive. Beforehand, they try to take on as much fat as they can to sustain themselves during their inactive periods. These animals can live for up to 10 years in captivity.

HIPPOPOTAMUS

TYPE OF ANIMAL:	Mammal
SWAHILI NAME:	*Kiboko*
SCIENTIFIC NAME:	*Hippopotamus amphibius*
SIZE:	The hippo measures 12 to 66 inches (30–168 cm) tall and 60 to 72 inches (152–183 cm) long; it weighs 585 to 825 pounds (266–375 kg).
WHERE IT LIVES:	Wet forests, streams, lakes, ponds, and swamps

The long-lived (40 to 50 years) hippo is a plant eater that can consume up to 88 pounds (40 kg) of grass a day. By day, these animals sleep and rest in the water; they are most active at night, when they search for food. They spend up to half their lives submerged. The word *hippopotamus*, by the way, means "river horse."

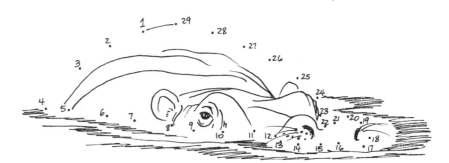

HYENA

TYPE OF ANIMAL: Mammal

SWAHILI NAME: *Fisi*

SCIENTIFIC NAME: *Crocuta crocuta*

SIZE: The hyena is about 45 inches (114 cm) long, plus a 13-inch (33 cm) tail; it weighs 82 to 190 pounds (37–86 kg).

WHERE IT LIVES: South of the Sahara Desert

With a life span of 12 to 25 years, the hyena is more closely related to moongooses and cats than it is to dogs. It eats meat: wildebeests, zebras, gazelles, buffalo, topi, eggs, and insects. It also eats some fruit. Hyenas have such powerful jaws and teeth that they can break open bones to get at the marrow. They can digest even bones, teeth, skin, and horns!

In ancient times, the Egyptians domesticated hyenas and also used them as a food source.

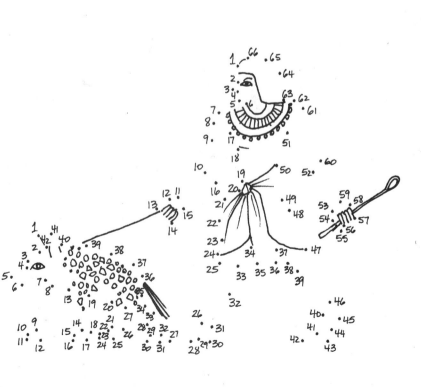

HYRAX

TYPE OF ANIMAL: Mammal

SWAHILI NAMES: *Pelele, wibari*

SCIENTIFIC NAMES: *Procavia capensis* (rock hyrax); *Heterohyrax brucei* (yellow spotted hyrax); *Dendrohyrax dorsalis* (tree hyrax)

SIZE: The hyrax is 12 inches (30 cm) tall at the shoulder, and weighs 5 to 9 pounds (2.3–4.1 kg).

WHERE IT LIVES: Dry savanna to dense rain forest

Although it's said to be the elephant's closest living relative, the hyrax looks more like a big guinea pig or rabbit. Very vocal animals, hyraxes make noises ranging from twitters, growls, and whistles all the way up to shrieks. They do most of their screaming at night while they're climbing trees. Their nocturnal cries are especially impressive: They can sound like squealing pigs or even a screaming child! Hyraxes eat plants, insects, lizards, and birds' eggs, and live for up to 12 years.

JACKAL

TYPE OF ANIMAL:	Mammal
SWAHILI NAME:	*Bweha*
SCIENTIFIC NAME:	*Canis aureus*
SIZE:	The jackal stands 15 to 20 inches (38–51 cm) tall at the shoulder; it weighs 15 to 35 pounds (6.8–15.9 kg).
WHERE IT LIVES:	Open and wooded savannas

This medium-sized mammal is an omnivore: It eats both meat and plants. Its diet includes antelope, gazelles, snakes, reptiles, insects, ground-dwelling birds, fruits, berries, and grasses. It generally lives for 10 to 12 years. Ancient Egyptians worshiped a jackal-headed god named Anubis, who was said to guide the souls of dead people to their judgment. Such beliefs are not surprising given this mammal's cleverness, its spooky howling, and its lifestyle as a nocturnal scavenger.

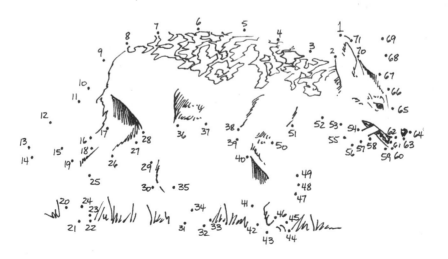

LEOPARD

TYPE OF ANIMAL: Mammal

SWAHILI NAME: *Chui*

SCIENTIFIC NAME: *Panthera pardus*

SIZE: The leopard measures 42 to 65 inches (107–165 cm) long, with a tail of 24 to 36 inches (61–91 cm); it weighs 65 to 175 pounds (30–80 kg).

WHERE IT LIVES: Rain forests, woodlands, plains, deserts, and shrubby areas in sub-Saharan Africa

Leopards are nocturnal animals: They hunt at night, then sleep during the day. They're swift runners, fine swimmers, and excellent at climbing trees (where they often hide their food). Prey includes a wide range of mammals, reptiles, birds, crabs, and fish. Leopards in captivity have lived for up to 21 years.

LION

TYPE OF ANIMAL:	Mammal
SWAHILI NAME:	*Simba*
SCIENTIFIC NAME:	*Panthera leo*
SIZE:	Measuring up to 10 feet (3 m) long, the lion weighs 275 to 425 pounds (125–193 kg).
WHERE IT LIVES:	Parts of Africa south of the Sahara Desert

Lions eat medium-sized animals such as zebras, gazelles, and wildebeests. As hunters, they fail more often than they succeed: Only 5 out of every 20 attempts they make to capture prey end with a kill! While they're hunting, lions can run up to 35 miles (56 km) per hour, but only for short distances. Their thunderous roars can be heard up to 5 miles (8 km) away. They live 15 to 20 years.

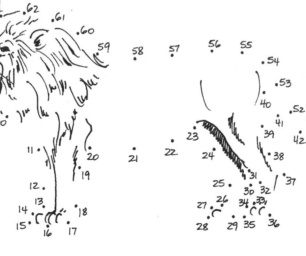

MARTIAL EAGLE

TYPE OF ANIMAL: Bird of prey

SWAHILI NAME: *Tai ngwilizi*

SCIENTIFIC NAME: *Polemaetus bellicosus*

SIZE: This eagle measures 33 inches (83 cm) tall, with a wingspan of 76 inches (193 cm); it weighs 14 pounds (6.5 kg).

WHERE IT LIVES: Savanna and thornbush areas of southern Africa

The largest eagle in Africa, the martial eagle can live for 25 years or more. It spends much of its time flying, soaring for hours on the wind without hunting; it can soar so high that it's almost invisible to the naked eye. When it does hunt, it eats reptiles (especially leguaans—also known as monitor lizards), game birds, and small antelopes.

MOUNTAIN GORILLA

TYPE OF ANIMAL:	Primate
SWAHILI NAME:	*Gorila, n'gagi*
SCIENTIFIC NAME:	*Gorilla berengei*
SIZE:	Standing up to 6 feet (1.8 m) tall, the mountain gorilla weighs 300 to 425 pounds (136–193 kg).
WHERE IT LIVES:	Rain forests and other dense forests

The largest living primate, the mountain gorilla eats a variety of plants. Favorites include wild celery, bamboo, thistles, stinging nettles, bedstraw, and certain fruits, all of which provide enough moisture that gorillas don't need to drink water. Gorillas spend their days wandering through home ranges of 10 to 15 square miles (26–39 sq km), feeding and resting. Each evening, they build new nests either in trees (where they're made from bent branches) or amid grasses on the ground. In captivity, mountain gorillas live as long as 53 years.

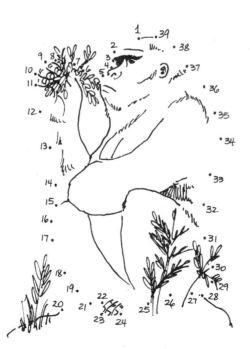

NILE CROCODILE

TYPE OF ANIMAL: Reptile

SWAHILI NAME: *Mamba*

SCIENTIFIC NAME: *Crocodylus niloticus*

SIZE: The Nile crocodile measures up to 20 feet, 5 inches (6.2 m) from head to tail; it weighs 500 to 1,650 pounds (225–730 kg).

WHERE IT LIVES: Throughout most of Africa, from Egypt to South Africa

The Nile crocodile is the largest of Africa's four crococile species. It can live 45 years in the wild, 80 years in captivity. Nile crocodiles are cold-blooded and need the sun to stay warm. While they often feed on animals that come to the water to drink—including zebras, hippos, wildebeests, porcupines, pangolins, and birds—their main food source is fish, including catfish. They also eat other crocodiles and carrion. They sometimes team up to hunt.

PANGOLIN

TYPE OF ANIMAL:	Mammal
SWAHILI NAME:	*Kakakuona*
SCIENTIFIC NAME:	*Manis temminckii*
SIZE:	The pangolin is 27 to 42 inches (69–107 cm) long; it weighs 30 to 40 pounds (14–18 kg).
WHERE IT LIVES:	Dense forest to forest savannas

The pangolin is sometimes called a scaly anteater—and indeed it does feed on ants and termites. It's sometimes also called an armadillo, but this is erroneous; the armadillo is a separate species found only in the Americas. Pangolin skin is covered with very heavy scales. The animal preens itself by scratching with its hind legs, lifting its scales to get at the skin. It also uses its tongue to remove insects from under its scales. It can live for 20 years.

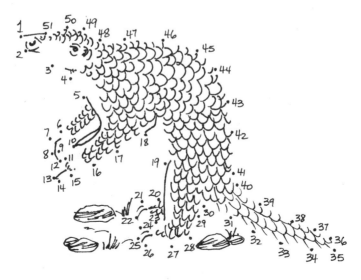

PORCUPINE

TYPE OF ANIMAL:	Mammal
SWAHILI NAME:	*Nungunungu*
SCIENTIFIC NAME:	*Hystrix cristata*
SIZE:	The porcupine is 33 inches (84 cm) long; it weighs 44 pounds (20 kg).
WHERE IT LIVES:	Porcupines are most common in hilly, rocky country, but they can adapt to most habitats.

The name *porcupine* means "quill pig." These animals eat roots, tubers, bark, and fallen fruit. They have a special fondness for cultivated root crops such as cassavas, potatoes, and carrots. While porcupines are vegetarians, their burrows are often littered with bones. Presumably, the animals bring them home to chew on for the calcium and other minerals they contain. Porcupines live for up to 20 years.

Porcupine quills are often used for all kinds of decoration and are considered good luck.

RATEL

TYPE OF ANIMAL:	Mammal
SWAHILI NAME:	*Nyegere*
SCIENTIFIC NAME:	*Mellivora capensis*
SIZE:	The ratel stands 10 inches (25 cm) tall and weighs 25 pounds (11 kg) or more.
WHERE IT LIVES:	Dense forest to open plains. The ratel can handle both dry and wet climates.

Also known as a honey badger, the ratel can live for 24 years. It eats meat, fruit, and carrion. Beehives are another favorite.

The ratel has an interesting relationship with the honeyguide, a kind of small bird. The honeyguide shows the ratel where a beehive can be found. The ratel gives off a smelly liquid to fumigate the hive, much the way human beekeepers use smoke. The ratel then scoops out the honeycomb while the honeyguide waits. When the mammal leaves, the bird eats the leftovers!

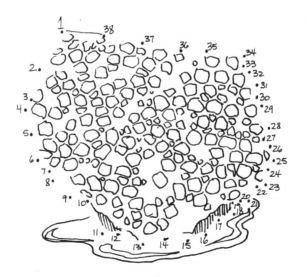

RHINOCEROS

TYPE OF ANIMAL: Mammal

SWAHILI NAME: *Kifaru*

SCIENTIFIC NAME: *Diceros bicornis*

SIZE: The rhino measures 5 to 7 feet (1.5–2.1 m) tall and 15 feet (4.6 m) long; it weighs 3,000 pounds (1,362 kg).

WHERE IT LIVES: Savannas

This second largest living land animal (after only the elephant) lives for 30 to 35 years and eats only plants. The rhino has a symbiotic relationship with oxpeckers, also called tick birds and, in Swahili, *askari wa kifaru*, which translates as "the rhino's guard." *Symbiotic* means that each species helps the other. In this case, the bird eats ticks it finds on the rhino and noisily warns it of danger.

SERVAL

TYPE OF ANIMAL:	Mammal
SWAHILI NAME:	*Mondo, kiskongo*
SCIENTIFIC NAME:	*Felix serval*
SIZE:	The serval stands 22 inches (56 cm) tall at the shoulder and weighs 30 to 40 pounds (14–18 kg).
WHERE IT LIVES:	Savannas

A small to medium-sized cat, the serval lives for up to 20 years. It eats birds, snakes, lizards, frogs, and insects—and it's notorious for raiding poultry flocks. Servals make a variety of noises, including a high-pitched cry that they use to call other servals. When they're angry, they snarl, growl, and spit. When they're happy, they purr.

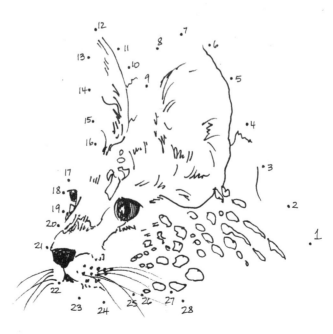

SITATUNGA

TYPE OF ANIMAL:	Mammal
SWAHILI NAME:	*Nzohe*
SCIENTIFIC NAME:	*Tragelaphus spekii*
SIZE:	The sitatunga stands 45 to 50 inches (114–127 cm) at the shoulder; it weighs 100 to 240 pounds (45–109 kg).
WHERE IT LIVES:	Thickly vegetated, muddy swamps and marshes

The sitatunga is the only amphibious antelope. It eats the plants it find in swamps and adjacent riverine forests. It will also eat fallen fruit and chew the bark of some trees and bushes. It lives for up to 19 years.

Effective but slow swimmers, sitatungas spend most of their time standing in water or on top of floating vegetation. Usually they're half submerged in the water, but in danger they will dive deeper and stay hidden until it's safe to come out.

SPRING HARE

TYPE OF ANIMAL:	Mammal
SWAHILI NAME:	*Kamendegere*
SCIENTIFIC NAME:	*Pedestes capensis*
SIZE:	The spring hare is 17 inches (43 cm) long and weighs 7 to 8 pounds (3.2–3.6 kg).
WHERE IT LIVES:	Dry savannas

The spring hare looks like a tiny kangaroo, but it's really a rodent. It eats the stems, roots, and sprouts of many plants, as well as herbs and the fruit of several shrubs. In captivity, it lives for up to 8 years. It's nocturnal, and at night its eyes reflect a deep reddish color.

THOMSON'S GAZELLE

TYPE OF ANIMAL: Mammal

SWAHILI NAME: *Swala tomi*

SCIENTIFIC NAME: *Gazella thomsonii*

SIZE: The Thomson's gazelle stands 22 to 26 inches (56–66 cm) at the shoulder; it weighs 33 to 55 pounds (15–25 kg).

WHERE IT LIVES: Open plains and grasslands

Nicknamed the tommy, the Thomson's gazelle is smaller than its relative, the Grant's gazelle. It can live for more than 10 years. Although grasses make up about 90 percent of the tommy's diet in the dry season, it also eats seeds and browses on shrubs. Its horns measure 18 to 32 inches (46–81 cm) long!

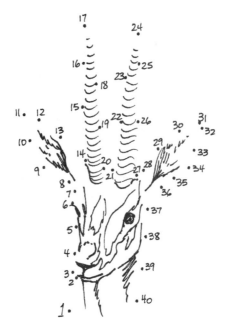

VERVET MONKEY

TYPE OF ANIMAL:	Primate
SWAHILI NAME:	*Tumbili*
SCIENTIFIC NAME:	*Cercopithecus aethiops*
SIZE:	This monkey is 18 to 26 inches (46–66 cm) long and weighs 7 to 17 pounds (3.2–7.7 kg).
WHERE IT LIVES:	Woodlands, savannas, and high bush

The small, black-faced vervet monkey has lived for 24 years in captivity. Leaves and young shoots make up most of its diet, but it also eats bark, flowers, fruit, bulbs, roots, and grass seeds. This is supplemented by insects, grubs, eggs, baby birds, and sometimes rodents and hares. Vervets hardly ever drink water.

Vervets rarely venture farther than about 1,500 feet (457 m) from trees, since they are vulnerable to many predators. Chirping and chittering are their most common noises, but they will scream and squeal when in danger.

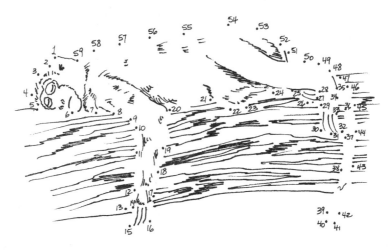

WARTHOG

TYPE OF ANIMAL: Mammal

SWAHILI NAME: *Ngiri*

SCIENTIFIC NAME: *Phacocoerus aethiopicus*

SIZE: The warthog is 30 inches (76 cm) tall at the shoulder; it weighs 120 to 150 pounds (55–68 kg).

WHERE IT LIVES: Open grasslands and savannas

The warthog is related to the pig and lives about 15 years. It is mainly a grazer, and has an unusual habit of kneeling on its hairy, padded knees to eat short grass. It also uses its snout and tusks to dig for bulbs, tubers, and roots during the dry season.

Lions and leopards are the warthog's chief enemies. To protect itself, a warthog will sometimes slide backward into a hole, putting it into position to use its fearsome tusks against the attacker.

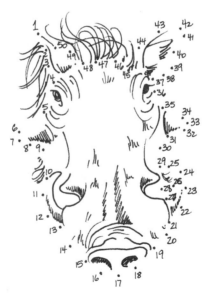

WILDEBEEST

TYPE OF ANIMAL: Mammal

SWAHILI NAME: *Nyumbu ya montu*

SCIENTIFIC NAME: *Connochaetes taurinus*

SIZE: The wildebeest measures 50 to 58 inches (127–147 cm) high at the shoulder; it weighs 265 to 600 pounds (120–272 kg).

WHERE IT LIVES: Open bush savannas and short grass plains

A type of antelope, wildebeests live for up to 20 years. They're strictly grazers, and short grass is their favorite. They cannot go without water for more than a few days. Wildebeests often migrate from area to area in large groups, following the seasons.

When neighboring bulls meet at the edges of their territories, they engage in a "challenge," which includes pawing the ground, bucking, snorting, and fighting.

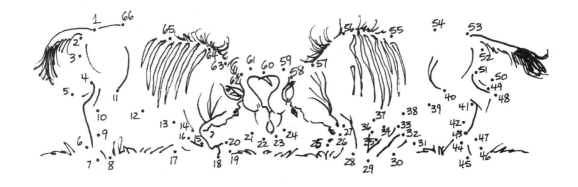

ZEBRA

TYPE OF ANIMAL: Mammal

SWAHILI NAME: *Punda milia*

SCIENTIFIC NAMES: *Equus grevyi* (Grevy's zebra); *E. burchelli* (plains zebra); *E. zebra* (mountain zebra)

SIZE: The zebra stands 47 to 57 inches (120–145 cm) tall and weighs 660 to 880 pounds (300–400 kg).

WHERE IT LIVES: Wooded areas and grassland habitats

Relatives of the horse, zebras in captivity have been known to live for 40 years. They eat grass, and they'll even eat dried-out grass so long as they have access to water as well. By the way, no two zebras are exactly alike; their stripe patterns are as unique as human fingerprints!

Zebras have also been used, like horses, to pull two-wheeled carts.

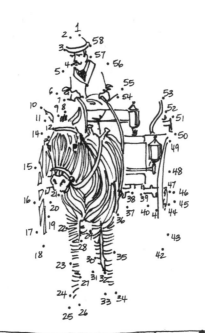

INDEX

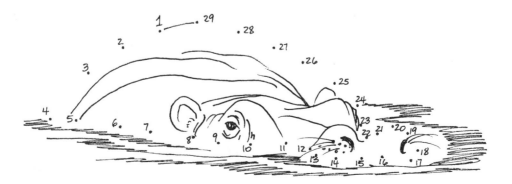